The Musical Marvel

Written by Nadine Cowan
Illustrated by Nadine Cowan and Katie Crumpton

Collins

Chapter 1

Olivia winced as a mangled *yelp* escaped from her violin and floated around the hall.

"Sorry," she mumbled.

Ms Orlov stopped playing the piano abruptly and slid her spectacles back up her nose.

"That's quite all right, Olivia, perhaps we'll stop there. We only have one week left until the show. Remember to practise the Joseph Bologne, Chevalier de Saint-Georges piece!"

Olivia closed the clasp on her violin case.

"That last part is difficult to get right," she said to her best friend, Aniyah.

"Tell me about it," Aniyah replied. "If I could, I'd tell the composer to make it easier."

Olivia nodded. "My head hurts just thinking about the show."

"Let's go to Blue Mahoes and play the Ludi game," Aniyah said.

"Finally, something I'm great at!" smiled Olivia.

Blue Mahoes was Aniyah and her cousin EJ's family restaurant. It served the best Caribbean meals in London.

"What took you so long?" said EJ, as the girls arrived. A steamy wave of red pea soup with dumplings wafted from the kitchen.

"Practice ran over," Aniyah replied.

"Well, I've got the Ludi board all set up. Come on, let's play!" said EJ.

The Ludi game was a family heirloom, and every time they played something magical happened. Etched on the side of the wooden board were the words:

Roll double six, or double three,

let's learn about your history.

EJ released the dice. They tumbled down and ricocheted off the side of the board.

"Five and two," announced Aniyah, before scooping them up. She shook the dice and rolled double three.

A puff of iridescent smoke emitted from the board.

"Here we goooo!" yelled EJ, as a tornado appeared, forming a wormhole that pulled them in.

The first thing Aniyah noticed was the smell of lavender and orange flower in the air.

The first thing she heard was EJ.

"Ha! You both have funny hair, and silly outfits," he laughed. "You look like a pair of cockatoos covered in confetti!"

Aniyah and Olivia glanced at each other and then back at EJ, before erupting into hysterical laughter.

"Have you seen yourself?" asked Aniyah.

"What's so funny!?" EJ turned round to look at his reflection in the window. A cloud of white dust fell from his head.

"That's a very nice wig, EJ," Olivia joked.

It was extravagant, with corkscrew curls tied back into an ornate bow. EJ's jaw dropped further as he looked at himself from head to toe. Large ruffles spilled out like a waterfall from a powdery pink waistcoat. It matched a long-tailed jacket bordered with gold embroidery.

"I particularly like the tights," Aniyah smirked.

EJ was wearing silk stockings over his trousers, which were decorated with bows. He lifted his foot to inspect the high heel on one of the leather shoes, which had a gleaming brooch.

Aniyah and Olivia's wigs had big curls, which cascaded beneath hats decorated with flowers and feathers.

"This is so uncomfortable!" said Aniyah.

"And itchy!" said Olivia. The silk brocade jacket had a panel of jewels, ribbons and pearls, and was pinned to the dress beneath. She held up her sleeve. "It looks like I'm wearing my grandma's doilies!"

"Where are we?" asked EJ, looking up at the grand building in front of them. They were standing beneath a portico overlooking a grand courtyard which was filled with ornate sculptures.

"I'm not sure," said Olivia. As she stepped back to get a better look at their surroundings, there was a loud thud as her shoe hit something.

"What's that?" asked Aniyah.

There were two odd-shaped boxes on the ground.

"They look like our violin cases," said Olivia, bending over them. She flipped one of the lids open to reveal what was inside.

Aniyah and EJ peered over Olivia's shoulder.

"It *is* a violin!" said Aniyah.

Suddenly, they heard footsteps approaching,

"*Excusez moi!*" said a man, as he strode past purposefully. Just before he reached the arched doors of the building, he spun around and pointed at the violins.

"You! You're here!"

Chapter 2

Aniyah, EJ and Olivia looked at each other in confusion. "Us?"

The man's face lit up. "Finally, you have arrived! My replacements!" He was slim and athletic and wore a wig like EJ's.

"Your what?" asked Aniyah.

"We have an audience with Queen Marie Antionette in a few hours. The Queen is on her way from the Palace of Versailles. This is a very important performance, as she will decide whether I become director of the Paris Opéra, but some of my musicians have not shown up."

"And you want us to play?" asked Olivia in disbelief. "Who are you?"

"*I* am Joseph Bologne, Chevalier de Saint-Georges. I have been the director of the Concert des Amateurs orchestra for three years – since 1773."

He looked them up and down. "You're younger than I was expecting, but I too started out as a young musician, and I suppose I've met many young prodigies. You're English?"

"Yes," said EJ.

"Welcome to Hôtel de Soubise, Paris," Joseph smiled.

"So, we're in France, in 1776!" whispered Aniyah to Olivia and EJ.

Joseph headed towards the entrance of the building. "Come, follow me," he said. "We have so much to do!"

"I'm EJ and this is my cousin, Aniyah, and our friend Olivia," said EJ.

"*Enchanté!*" nodded Joseph.

As they walked through Hôtel de Soubise, Aniyah looked up and saw grand chandeliers and powder-blue ceilings.

"Look at the paintings," she whispered to the others.

"Look at that sword!" said EJ.

There were servants rushing about, making sure everything was perfect. A maid was scrubbing the floors, and another was polishing a huge mirror.

Aniyah spotted a third maid leaning on the grand staircase banister, catching her breath.

"I wouldn't mind swapping dresses but not jobs," said Olivia.

There was the sound of instruments being tuned as they approached a set of gold doors. Joseph pushed them open, and sunlight crept out and danced over their faces. They found themselves in a grand hall, where an orchestra had assembled. There were violinists, cellists and double-bass players on one side, and musicians with flutes, clarinets, trumpets, horns, oboes and bassoons nearby.

"Joseph Bologne!" Olivia said.

"I know, he introduced himself already," Aniyah replied.

"No, no, it's *the* Joseph Bologne. As in Joseph Bologne whose music we're supposed to learn for the summer show next week!" said Olivia. "Now's your chance!"

Aniyah looked confused. "For what?"

"To tell him to make it easier!" Olivia said.

But before they could say anything, Joseph introduced them to the other violinists.

"We usually have 40 violinists, but as you can see, a lot of them haven't shown up."

"What shall I do?" EJ asked.

"Can you play an instrument?" asked Joseph.

EJ scratched his head. "Well, I reckon I could play the drums. I'm pretty good at banging on the pots and pans – "

Joseph raised an eyebrow.

"I'm great at rapping and street dance," EJ boasted.

"Really?" Aniyah said.

EJ raised his hand to his mouth as though he was holding an invisible mic.

"Lyrics hotter than Jerk chicken spice,
Nice, like gravy all over the rice
It's me ... the greatest MC,
EJ from Hackney – "

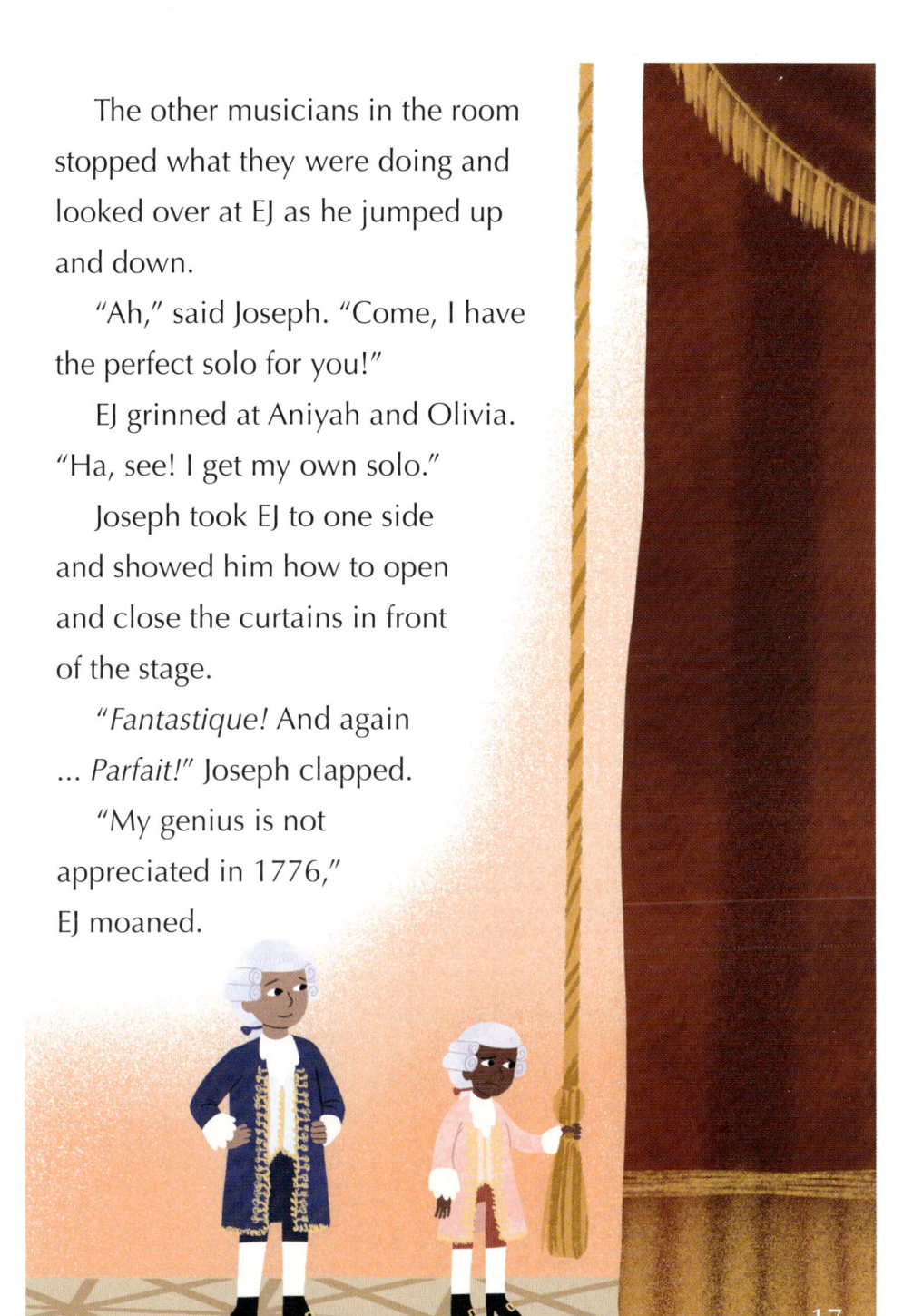

The other musicians in the room stopped what they were doing and looked over at EJ as he jumped up and down.

"Ah," said Joseph. "Come, I have the perfect solo for you!"

EJ grinned at Aniyah and Olivia. "Ha, see! I get my own solo."

Joseph took EJ to one side and showed him how to open and close the curtains in front of the stage.

"*Fantastique!* And again ... *Parfait!*" Joseph clapped.

"My genius is not appreciated in 1776," EJ moaned.

Joseph returned to Aniyah and Olivia. "Let me show you your part."

The girls took out the violins.

"Like this," said Joseph, as he readjusted Olivia's hand, and placed Aniyah's bow. "You must make every note count!"

Olivia's hand quivered as she tried desperately to hit the right notes. Once again, a mangled *yelp* escaped and fled around the hall.

"Relax your shoulders, flex your wrist, and bring your bow to the middle. Become the music, connect with it and feel it from deep within!" instructed Joseph.

Joseph picked up a violin, closed his eyes, and began to play. Olivia, Aniyah and EJ watched with wonder.

When Joseph finished, he signalled for the orchestra to begin. Olivia took a deep breath and tried again. The notes flowed from the violin.

Joseph smiled. "Bravo, Olivia!"

Suddenly there was a cracking sound, and one of the large crystal chandeliers fell from the ceiling, shattering on the floor with an almighty crash.

Chapter 3

Everyone rushed to look at the damage. Crystal shards were scattered across the floor like bright jewels.

"It's just an unfortunate accident," Joseph said, but the children could see he looked worried. "Let's take a break, and get some fresh air," Joseph continued. "The maids will clear it up."

The air wasn't very fresh. *It smells,* thought EJ, as he followed Joseph, Olivia and Aniyah through the courtyard.

"Do we really think that was an accident?" he whispered to Aniyah and Olivia.

Aniyah shrugged her shoulders. "I'm not sure."

Just then, they arrived at some stables.

"Do you ride?" Joseph asked them.

"I've had lessons," Olivia replied.

"I'm an excellent rider," Joseph told them. "I can also shoot, fence, swim and skate! I joined the King's Guard in 1761 after graduating from the fencing academy."

"That's a lot!" said Aniyah.

"I'm a man of many talents," Joseph agreed. "Coming to France changed the course of my life, and I seize every opportunity that comes my way. Becoming the artistic director of the Paris Opéra would be a dream come true."

"So, you haven't always lived in France?" asked Aniyah.

Joseph shook his head. "I was born in the West Indies, on the island of Guadeloupe."

"My family is from the West Indies too," Aniyah replied.

"My mother, Nanon, is a Senegalese woman who was once enslaved, and my father was a planter of French origin. When I was a young child, my father brought me to France because he thought I would have a better life. I went to the finest schools and mixed with the nobility," Joseph recalled.

"I want to be the best at everything I do because not everyone has accepted me due to my heritage and the colour of my skin."

"I wish I could play the violin like you," said Olivia.

Joseph smiled. "You must start from somewhere; I started off as first violin and worked my way up to director. Keep practising, and in time you'll be better than me!"

He looked back at the hotel. "The guests will be arriving soon, let's hope no more chandeliers fall from the ceiling!"

But when they got back to the hall, some of the musicians were looking upset.

"What is it now?" asked Joseph.

"Our violins! Some of them have been tampered with. The strings have been cut!" replied one of the musicians.

Aniyah and Olivia rushed over to their cases and opened them.

"Ours are OK," said Aniyah.

Just then a footman appeared. "Her Majesty the Queen has arrived!"

Joseph looked determined. "It's too late to find replacements. We'll have to do the performance with what we have!"

Chapter 4

Everyone could hear the guests filling the hall. EJ, Aniyah and Olivia peeped through the curtain.

"Cutting the violin strings was *definitely* not an accident," Aniyah said.

"Let's investigate later," Olivia replied.

Joseph appeared beside them. "The queen has the biggest dress and hairstyle," he said. "EJ, get ready with the curtain. Everyone else, follow my lead!"

Suddenly, everyone was silent. "Positions, everyone!" Joseph whispered. He gave EJ the signal, and EJ tugged on the rope. The curtains began to rise, and the crowd applauded politely. Joseph took a bow, raised the baton in his hand, and the orchestra began to play. Olivia relaxed her shoulders, flexed her wrist, and raised her bow.

The show was a success! The orchestra gave a sensational performance, which brought the audience to its feet. Joseph gave a final bow as a round of applause filled the hall.

"What happens now?" asked Olivia.

"Now it's time for the banquet!" Joseph announced.

"Yes!" EJ grinned.

The dining hall was just as grand as the rest of Hôtel de Soubise.

There was an elaborate spread with hollowed pumpkins filled with soup and meringue, as well as extravagant cakes, pastries and desserts.

"Try this," said Joseph, reaching for a glazed, hand-painted porcelain jar. Aniyah dipped her spoon into a runny substance, it was sweet.

"It's made with fruits, and cream; isn't it the finest ice-cream you've ever tasted?" asked Joseph.

Well, it's not exactly a double chocolate fudge brownie sundae with sprinkles, that's for sure, thought Aniyah.

EJ was eyeing up one of the large cakes, when he spotted something strange. One of the servants took out a vial with liquid from his waistcoat, lifted the cloche on the serving tray and poured the vial's contents into the dish.

Perhaps it's some sort of seasoning or dressing, EJ thought.

The waiter brought the dish to Joseph and lifted the cloche. Steam rose from the plate.

"Mmm … breaded pâté," said Joseph.

Olivia made a face. Whatever breaded pâté was, it didn't look like anything she wanted to eat.

EJ couldn't shake the uneasy feeling that something wasn't quite right. When Joseph began to lift the fork to his mouth, EJ jumped up and shouted.

"No!"

Chapter 5

Joseph froze, and so did the other guests. The murmur of conversation mingled with laughter came to a halt.

"That servant put something in your food!" announced EJ. Everyone gasped and looked over. The servant shoved one of the maids out of the way and ran out of the door.

Joseph shot up from his chair and ran after him. EJ ran around the table and followed Joseph; Aniyah and Olivia weren't too far behind.

By the time they'd caught up with him, the servant was halfway down the stairs. Joseph jumped onto the gold banister and slid down in pursuit. He landed on his feet before the servant reached the bottom of the stairs.

The servant tried to turn around, back up the stairs, but EJ, Aniyah and Olivia were blocking the way.

"Got you now!" EJ grinned.

The servant pulled a sword from its sheath, hidden beneath his jacket.

EJ stopped grinning. "Maybe not!"

In a flash, Joseph grabbed the sword that was on display.

The servant lunged towards Joseph, but Joseph cleverly side-stepped.

The percussion of metal echoed off the walls of the entrance hall as their swords clashed and locked. Joseph charged forward, overpowering his opponent, who dropped to the floor. Joseph disarmed him with astonishing agility, and the servant's sword came crashing down and slid across the polished floor.

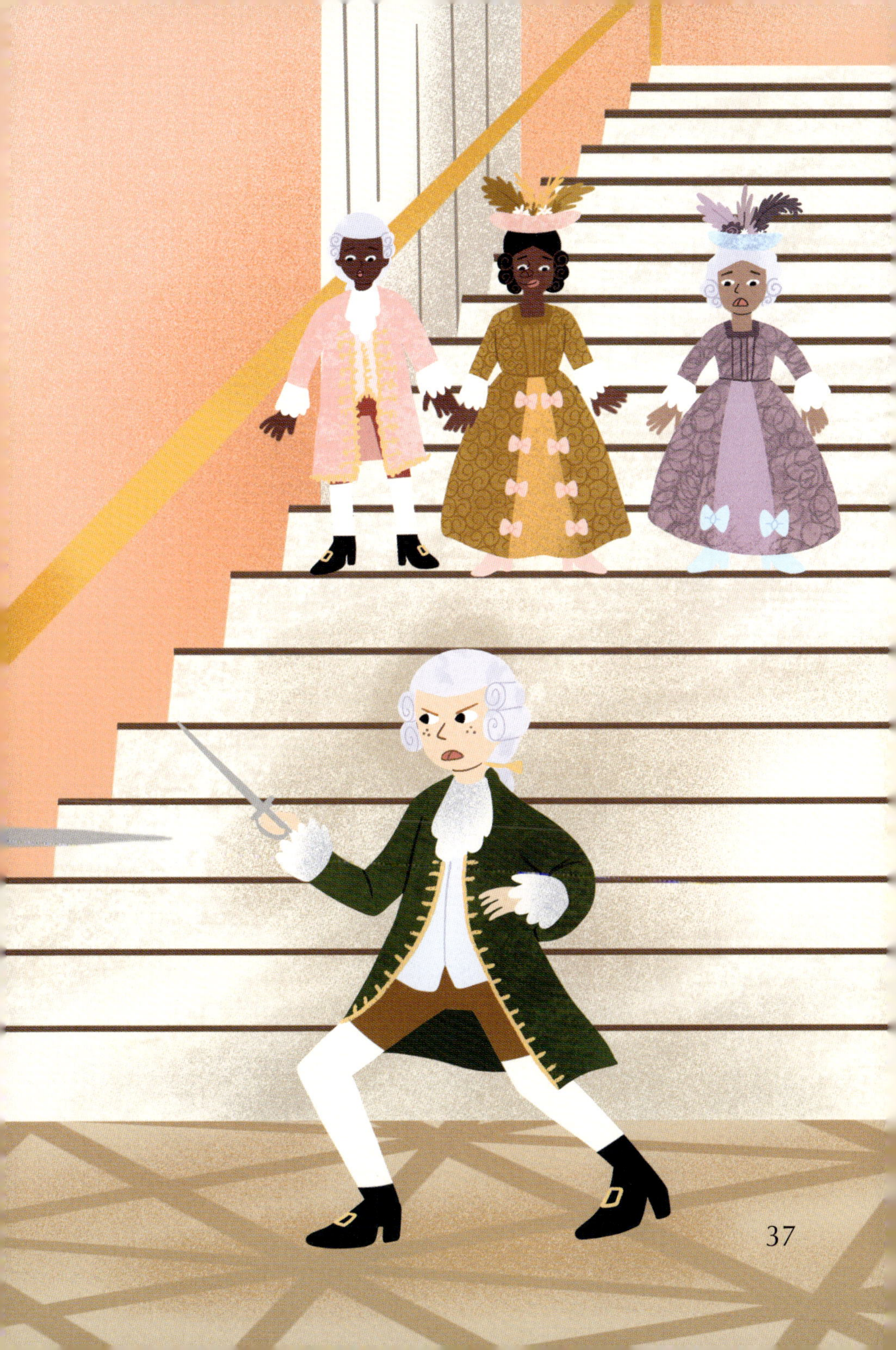

The servant squirmed frantically as Joseph's sword came flying towards his chest. But at the very last moment, Joseph swooped the sword upwards, and the servant's wig flew off.

The children gasped.

Amber curls toppled down the assailant's shoulders.

"That's not a man! That's the maid we saw on the stairs earlier," said Aniyah.

"That's no maid!" said Joseph. "I recognise you! You're a dancer at the Royal Opéra. You keep company with Marie-Madeleine Guimard!"

EJ turned to the others. "Marie Grimsby who?"

Joseph laid his sword down. "What's the meaning of this? Why do you mean me harm?"

"You'll never be the artistic director of the Paris Opéra," snarled the woman.

"Did you cut the violin strings?" asked Olivia.

The woman gave them an unpleasant grin. "Yes! And I caused the chandelier to fall, too."

"But why?" asked Aniyah.

"Remember when I told you not everyone accepts me because of my heritage and the colour of my skin?" explained Joseph. "Some people at the Paris Opéra are opposed to me becoming director."

"I'll never work for you!" shouted the woman.

"That's a shame, because Joseph's an amazing musician," said Olivia.

Some of the guards who had arrived with Queen Marie Antoinette came running into the entrance hall.

"Unhand me, let me go!" wailed the woman, as the guards led her away.

Chapter 6

"I can't believe she sabotaged the violins," EJ started.

"*And* caused the chandelier to crash," continued Aniyah.

"Then she tried to poison Joseph!" Olivia finished.

Joseph overhead them. "But thanks to you, I will live to see another day!"

The queen appeared.

"The performance was marvellous, Joseph; I eagerly anticipate what you come up with next," she declared.

"For my next piece, I've been inspired by my young friend EJ here, Your Majesty. It's like poetry with a melody –" Joseph winked at EJ.

"My name's Joseph Bologne, Chevalier,
I'm a handsome young man with marvellous hair!
Master of a … multitude of things.
A virtuoso on the strings …"

Suddenly, a magical cloud appeared above their heads, made a tornado that formed a wormhole and pulled Aniyah, Olivia and EJ in. They were back at Blue Mahoes.

"Wow, we had a music lesson with the composer himself!" said Aniyah.

"Ms Orlov won't believe it," Olivia replied, smiling.

"I'm glad I don't have to wear those heels. But most of all …" said EJ, patting his head, "… my awesome hair is back to normal!"

The day of the concert had arrived. Olivia and Aniyah watched as the audience poured through the doors, down the rows and into their seats. They saw their parents and waved.

Olivia felt a pit form in her stomach as she took her position in the junior orchestra and perched her chin upon the violin. Then she heard Joseph's voice in her head: "Become the music, connect with it and feel it from deep within."

And so, she did just that.

The orchestra

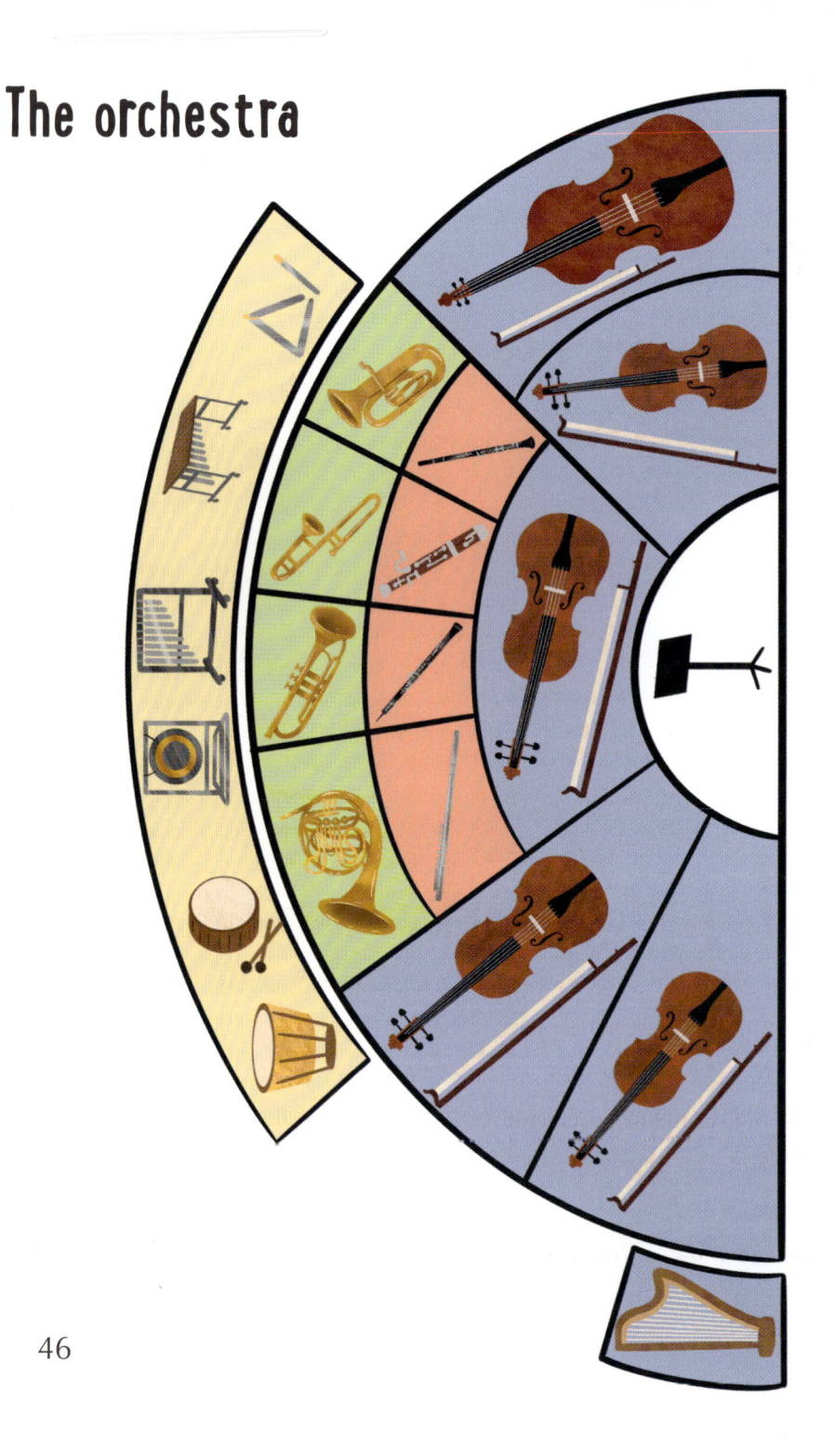

REAL PEOPLE

Joseph Bologne, Chevalier de Saint-Georges
1745-1799

Joseph Bologne was born on the island of Guadeloupe, and brought to France by his father, who was a wealthy plantation owner. He studied literature, music and mathematics at school, and enrolled at a fencing academy. Joseph moved to Paris and excelled at everything he did: swimming, shooting, dancing and ice skating. Joseph knew Queen Marie Antoinette well, and taught her music, but he never became director of the Paris Opéra.

Ideas for reading

Written by Gill Matthews
Primary Literacy Consultant

Reading objectives:
- check that the text makes sense to them, discussing their understanding and explaining the meaning of words in context
- draw inferences such as inferring characters' feelings, thoughts and motives from their actions, and justifying inferences with evidence
- identify main ideas drawn from more than one paragraph and summarising these

Spoken language objectives:
- use relevant strategies to build their vocabulary
- maintain attention and participate actively in collaborative conversations, staying on topic and initiating and responding to comments
- use spoken language to develop understanding through speculating, hypothesising, imagining and exploring ideas

Curriculum links: Relationship education: Respectful relationships

Interest words: excusez moi, enchanté, fantastique, parfait

Build a context for reading

- Ask children to look closely at the front cover and to describe what they see.
- Discuss what the title means to them.
- Read the back-cover blurb.

Understand and apply reading strategies

- Read pages 2–4 aloud, using punctuation, meaning and dialogue to help you to read with appropriate expression. Discuss the techniques that you have demonstrated.
- Discuss any other books the children have read that featured the characters EJ, Olivia and Aniyah. Encourage them to predict where the children might be transported to in this story.
- Children can read pages 5–9 aloud, using the techniques that you demonstrated.
- Explore the clues that might help to work out where and when the three characters have ended up.